peak zero

Alan Brighouse
David Godber
Peter Patilla

(relating to National Curriculum Levels 2 and 3)

Nelson

Thomas Nelson and Sons Ltd
Nelson House Mayfield Road
Walton-on-Thames Surrey
KT12 5PL UK

Nelson Blackie
Wester Cleddens Road
Bishopbriggs
Glasgow G64 2NZ UK

Thomas Nelson Australia
102 Dodds Street
South Melbourne
Victoria 3205 Australia

Nelson Canada
1120 Birchmount Road
Scarborough Ontario
M1K 5G4 Canada

© **A. Brighouse, D. Godber, P. Patilla 1981, 1989**

Original edition 1981
This edition first published 1989

I(T)P Thomas Nelson is an International
Thomson Publishing Company

I(T)P is used under licence

ISBN 0-17-421557-6
NPN 9 8 7

Printed in Hong Kong

Filmset in Nelson Teaching Alphabet
by Mould Type Foundry Ltd
Dunkirk Lane Leyland England

Design Sharon Platt, Linda Reed

Photography Chris Ridgers

Illustration Amanda Hall

Contents

Number and Algebra

1. $7 + 4$ 2. $6 + 9$ 3. $8 + 8$ 4. $7 + 5$

5. $3 + 9$ 6. $4 + 5$ 7. $9 + 8$ 8. $7 + 6$

9. $0 + 9$ 10. $5 + 8$ 11. $4 + 7$ 12. $6 + 2$

13. $5 + 9$ 14. $9 + 9$ 15. $3 + 6$ 16. $7 + 8$

17. $14 - 7$ 18. $18 - 9$ 19. $11 - 5$ 20. $15 - 8$

21. $12 - 4$ 22. $17 - 9$ 23. $16 - 7$ 24. $13 - 8$

25. $4 + \square = 10$

26. $15 - \square = 6$ 27. $\square + 8 = 12$

28. $15 - \square = 7$ 29. $6 + \square = 13$

30. $\square - 7 = 4$ 31. $\square + 9 = 15$

32. $11 - \square = 2$ 33. $\square + 5 = 14$

SOLD OUT

4

Each clown had 10 cups.

1. How many did the red clown break?

2. Which clown broke the most cups?

3. How many cups were broken altogether?

4. How many more did the yellow clown break than the green clown?

Number line to 100

1. Start at 8.
   Count on in tens to 98.
   Write your answers
   like this: 8, 18, 28,

2. Start at 4.
   Count on in tens to 94.

3. Start at 7.
   Count on in tens to 97.

4. Start at 10.
   Count on in tens to 90.

5. Start at 93.
   Count back in tens to 3.

6. Start at 95.
   Count back in tens to 5.

7. Start at 89.
   Count back in tens to 9.

Counting sticks

Count out 14 sticks.

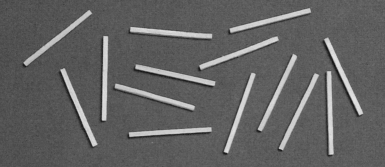

Make a bundle of 10 sticks.

14 = 1 bundle and 4 sticks

Make these into bundles of ten.

1. 17 sticks
2. 22 sticks
3. 29 sticks
4. 19 sticks
5. 30 sticks
6. 27 sticks
7. 32 sticks
8. 25 sticks
9. 28 sticks
10. 23 sticks
11. 33 sticks
12. 35 sticks

Here are 4 bundles of ten.
There are 40 sticks altogether.

How many sticks in each of these?

1.

2.

3.

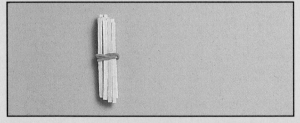

4.

5.

6.

7.

8.

Here are 2 bundles and 7 sticks.
There are 27 sticks altogether.

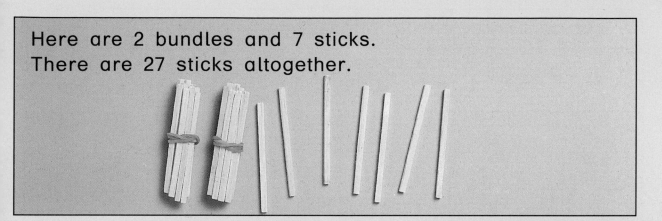

How many sticks in each of these?

1.

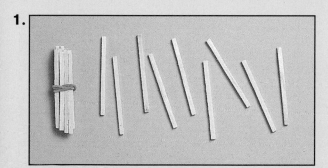

2.

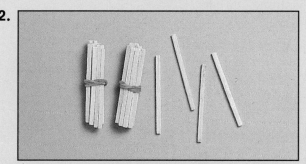

3.

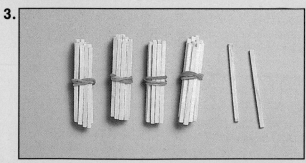

4.

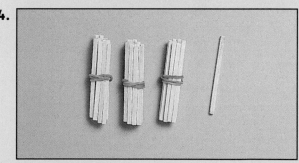

5.

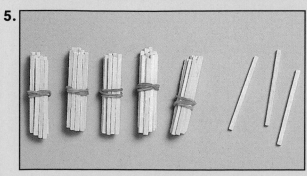

6.

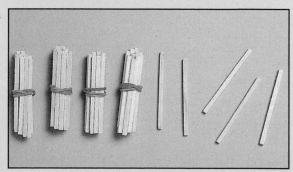

Shape and space

9 pin geoboard, elastic bands, spotty paper

All these shapes have a square corner.

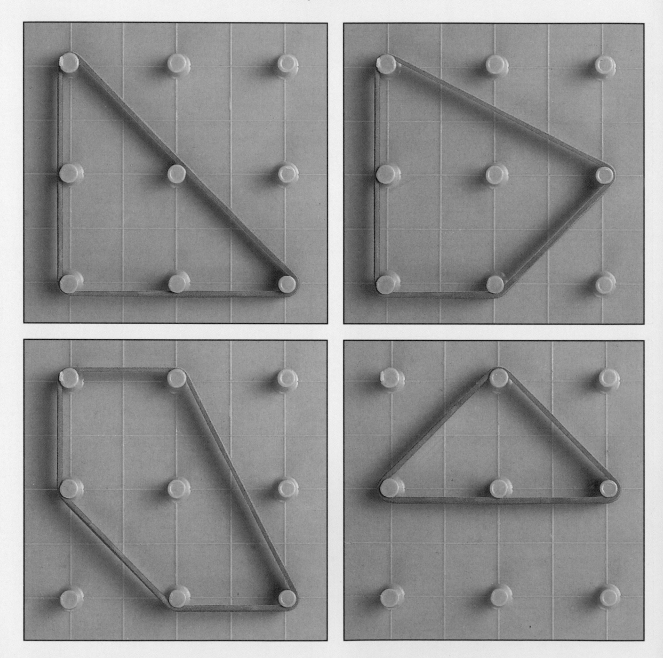

Make some other shapes with square corners.

9 pin geoboard, elastic bands, spotty paper

These shapes have no square corners.

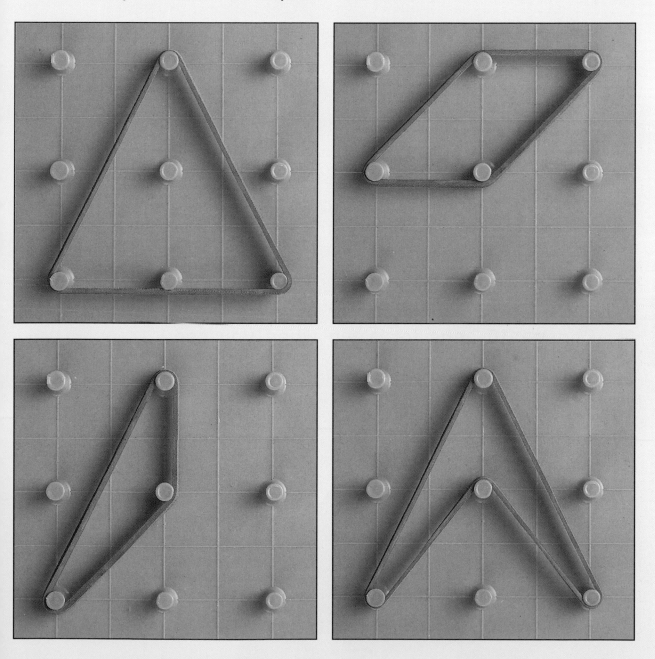

Make some other shapes with no square corners.

Number and Algebra

Base 10 apparatus, dice

Target 40

A game for 2 or more players.

You need

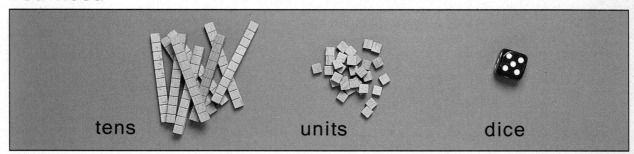

tens   units   dice

Rules

1. Take turns to roll the dice.
2. Take the same number of units as the dice shows.
3. Change 10 units for a ten when you can.

The winner

The winner is
the first to have
4 tens.

Base 10 apparatus

13 units can be changed to 1 ten 3 units.

13 = 1 ten 3 units

Change these units into tens and units.

1. 18 units
2. 20 units
3. 23 units

4. 27 units
5. 17 units
6. 30 units

7. 15 units
8. 28 units
9. 21 units

10. 19 units
11. 34 units
12. 29 units

Base 10 apparatus

A game for two or more players.

Start with 5 tens each.

Rules

1. Take turns to throw the dice.
2. Take away the number of units shown on the dice. (You might have to change one of your tens to do it.)

The winner
The winner is the first person to have none left.

Base 10 apparatus

Take away 8 units from each of these.
Write how many you have left.

1.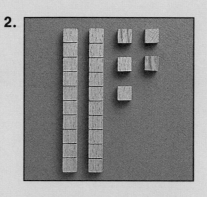

2.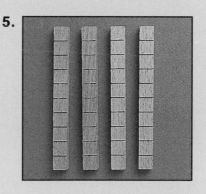

3.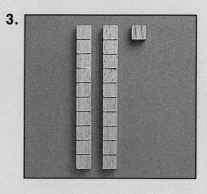

Take away 5 units from each of these.

4.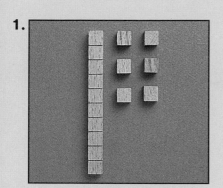

5.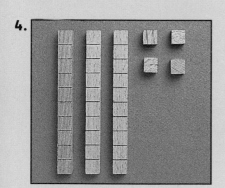

6.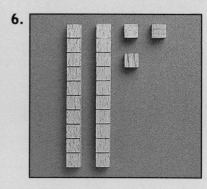

Take away 9 units from each of these.

7.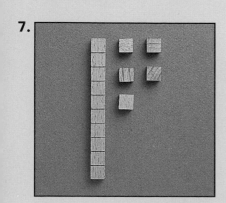

8.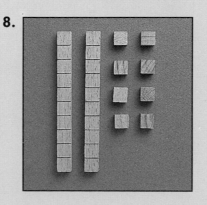

9.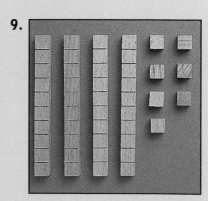

Measures

Metre stick

1 m

Measure the height of a table with the metre stick.

Now measure the width of the table.

Are you a good estimator?

Make a list of six items you can measure.
Estimate and measure the length of each one.
Measure in centimetres.

Item	Estimate	Measurement

Number and Algebra

Base 10 apparatus

Here is 1 ten 7 units.
It is written 17.

Write these numbers.

1.

2.

3.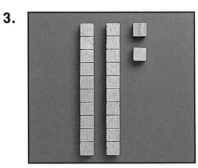

4.

5.

6.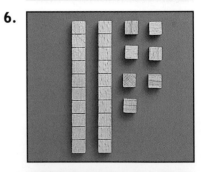

7.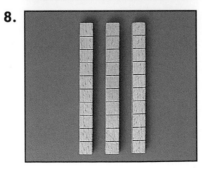

8.

9.

18

Base 10 apparatus

26 ———————————>

Draw these numbers.

1.

14 ——>

2.

17 ——>

3.

21 ——>

4.

15 ——>

5.

30 ——>

6.

24 ——>

7.

23 ——>

8.

40 ——>

Base 10 apparatus

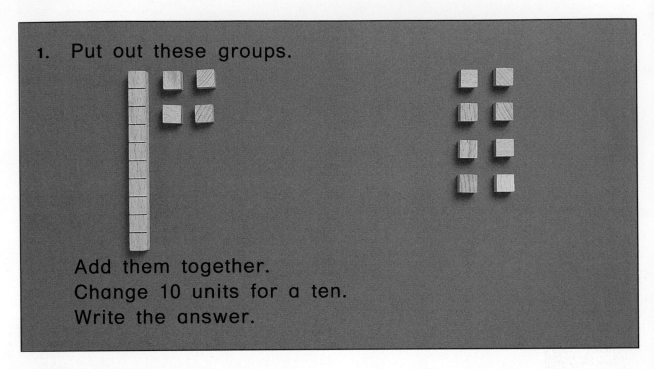

1. Put out these groups.

   Add them together.
   Change 10 units for a ten.
   Write the answer.

Do these in the same way.

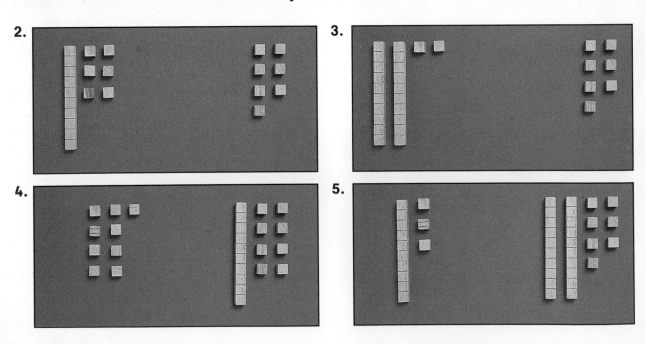

2.

3.

4.

5.

6.

7.

8.

9.

10.

11.

12.

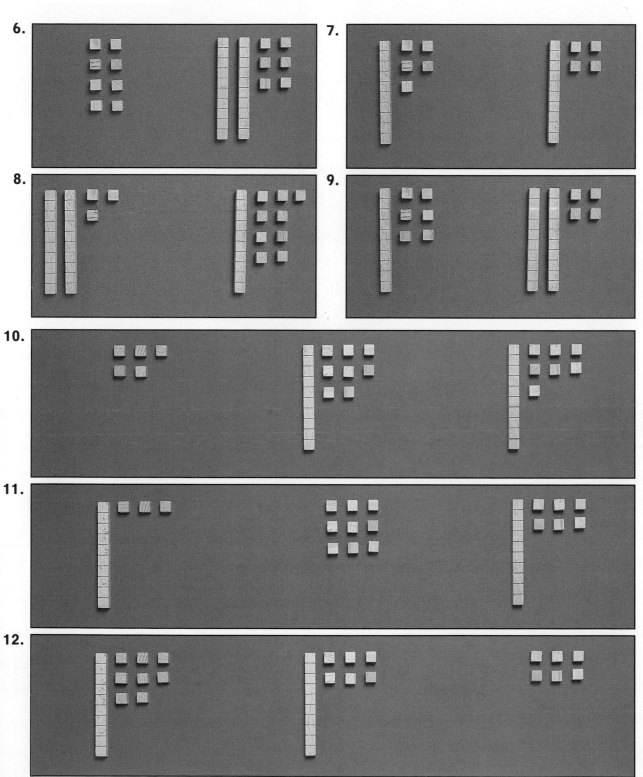

Measures

Kilogram weight

This is a kilogram.

Find things that are heavier than 1 kg.
Make a list of them.

Find things that are lighter than 1 kg.
Make a list of them.

Heavier than 1 kg	Lighter than 1 kg

How many of each of these weigh 1 kg?

Number and Algebra

T	U

Put 26 on your place value sheet.

Now put 15 on your place value sheet.

Add them together.
Change units for a ten.

Write it like this.

$$
\begin{array}{r}
2\ 6 \\
+\ 1\ 5 \\
\hline
4\ 1 \\
\hline
\end{array}
$$

24

Base 10 apparatus, place value sheet

Add each of these.

1.

T	U

2.

T	U

3.

T	U

4.

T	U

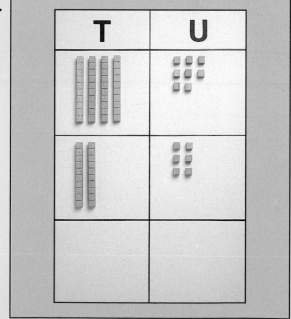

Base 10 apparatus, place value sheet

1.   3 8
   + 2 1
   _____

   _____

2.   3 6
   + 1 9
   _____

   _____

3.   2 3
   + 5 2
   _____

   _____

4.   4 7
   + 2 8
   _____

   _____

5.   2 3
   + 5 9
   _____

   _____

6.   3 0
   + 4 5
   _____

   _____

7.   2 8
   + 1 1
   _____

   _____

8.   3 8
   + 1 8
   _____

   _____

9.   4 7
   + 2 6
   _____

   _____

10.   3 5
   + 3 5
   _____

   _____

11.   4 3
   + 4 6
   _____

   _____

12.   2 1
   + 3 3
   _____

   _____

13.   5 6
   + 2 8
   _____

   _____

14.   2 2
   + 4 9
   _____

   _____

15.   3 6
   + 2 3
   _____

   _____

16.   2 9
   + 3 5
   _____

   _____

17.   5 1
   + 1 7
   _____

   _____

18.   4 6
   + 1 9
   _____

   _____

19.   1 3
   + 2 7
   _____

   _____

20.   2 5
   + 3 1
   _____

   _____

Base 10 apparatus, place value sheet

1.
```
   4 8
 + 3 2
 _____

 _____
```

2.
```
   2 4
 + 4 7
 _____

 _____
```

3.
```
   5 4
 + 2 0
 _____

 _____
```

4.
```
   2 1
 + 4 8
 _____

 _____
```

5.
```
   2 6
 + 1 9
 _____

 _____
```

6.
```
   1 9
 + 1 7
 _____

 _____
```

7.
```
   5 2
 + 2 8
 _____

 _____
```

8.
```
   3 7
 + 2 2
 _____

 _____
```

9.
```
   1 4
   3 9
 + 2 5
 _____

 _____
```

10.
```
   1 9
   4 4
 + 2 8
 _____

 _____
```

11.
```
   3 6
   1 4
 + 2 3
 _____

 _____
```

12.
```
   2 7
   4 7
 + 1 7
 _____

 _____
```

13.
```
   1 8
   2 5
 + 2 5
 _____

 _____
```

14.
```
   2 4
   1 8
 + 3 0
 _____

 _____
```

15.
```
   1 8
   3 8
 + 1 6
 _____

 _____
```

16.
```
   2 7
   2 9
 + 3 8
 _____

 _____
```

Write these numbers as words.

1.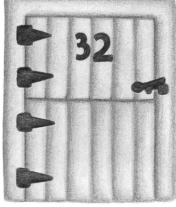

2.

3.

4.

5.

6.

Write these as numbers.

7. twenty

8. fifty-two

9. eighty-six

10. thirteen

11. nineteen

12. fifty-one

13. forty-seven

14. seventy-eight

15. eighty-four

16. thirty-five

17. sixty-nine

18. ninety-three

Calculator

Where will the rockets land?
Add the numbers in each rocket to find out.
Use a calculator to help you.

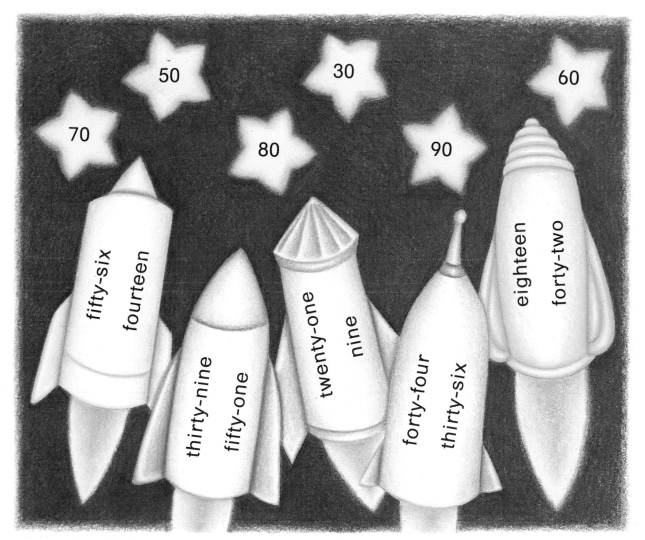

One of the stars has no rocket.
Draw a rocket.
Put numbers in it to make it land on that star.

Measures

Litre container

This holds 1 litre.

Find containers that hold less than 1 litre.
Make a list of them.

Find containers that hold more than 1 litre.
Make a list of them.

Hold less than 1 litre	Hold more than 1 litre

How many of each of these fill the litre jug?

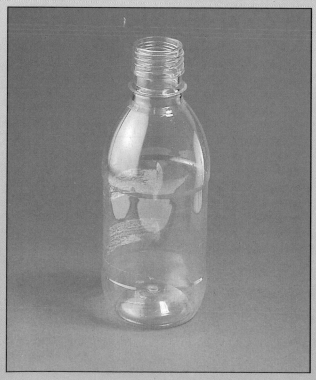

Number and Algebra

Both these show 32.

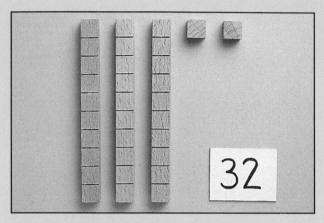 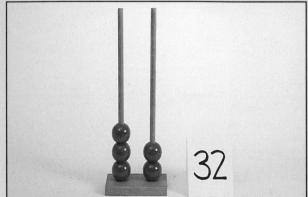

Show these on an abacus.

1.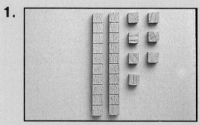

2.

3.

4.

5.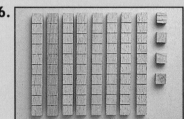

6.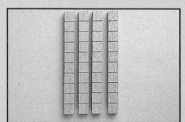

7.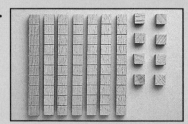

8.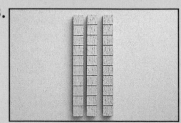

9.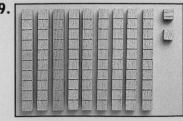

Rod abacus, abacus sheet

Write these as numbers.

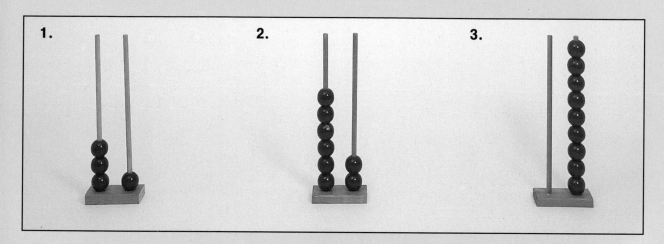

Write these as words.

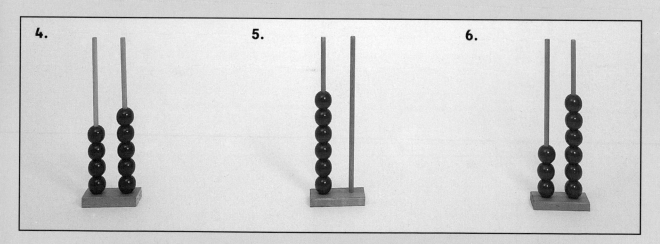

Show each of these numbers on an abacus.

7.	48	8.	18	9.	82	10.	41
11.	80	12.	7	13.	73	14.	94

33

Rod abacus

Write the numbers which are:

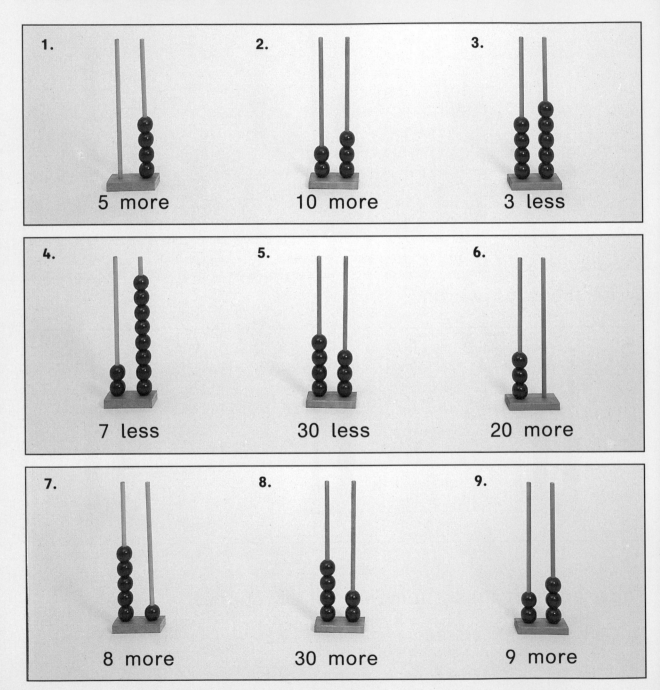

1. 5 more
2. 10 more
3. 3 less

4. 7 less
5. 30 less
6. 20 more

7. 8 more
8. 30 more
9. 9 more

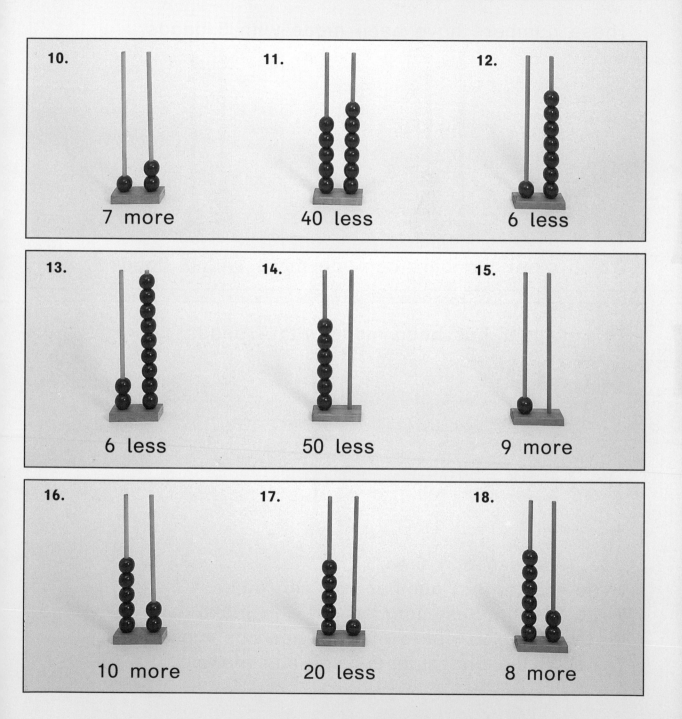

10. 7 more

11. 40 less

12. 6 less

13. 6 less

14. 50 less

15. 9 more

16. 10 more

17. 20 less

18. 8 more

Rod abacus

These numbers have been made with 3 beads.

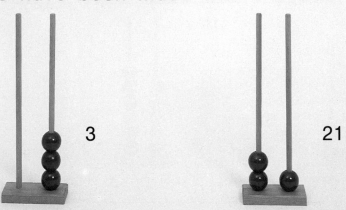

3   21

Which other numbers can you make with 3 beads?

This number has been made with 4 beads.

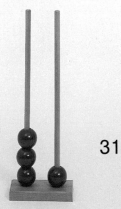

31

Use 4 beads each time.
Write the largest number you can make.
Write the smallest number you can make.
Write all the numbers over 20 you can make.
Write all the odd numbers you can make.

Rod abacus

What has been added?

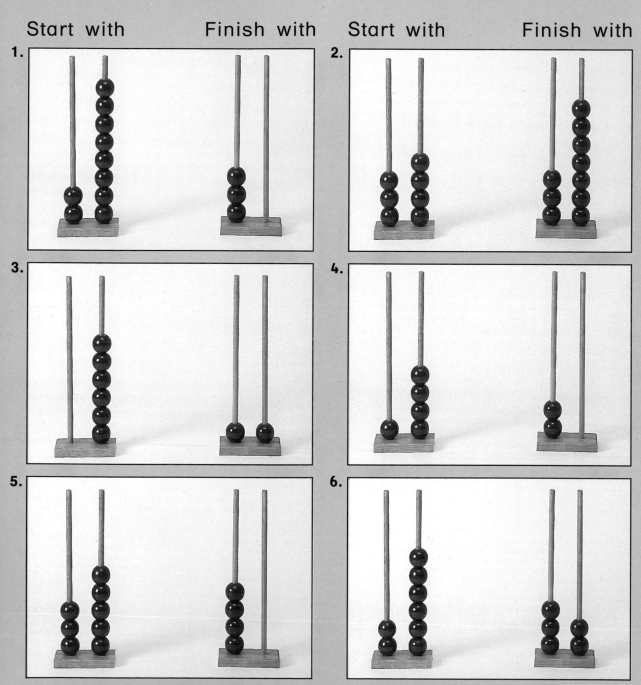

Which numbers do the letters point to?

1.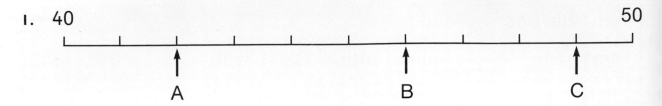

2.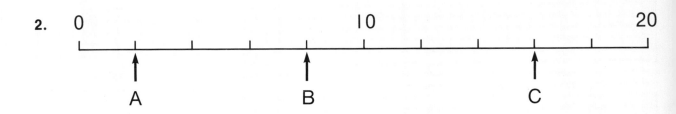

3.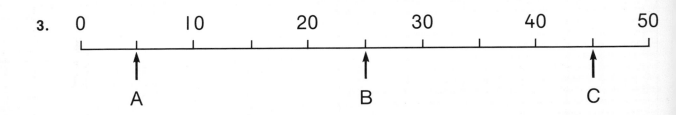

4.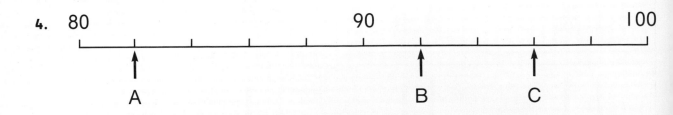

5.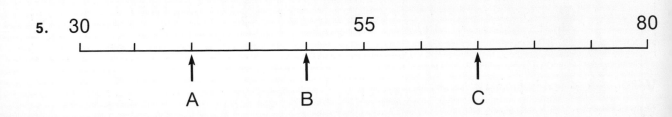

Find the score for each person.

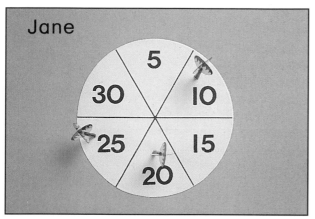

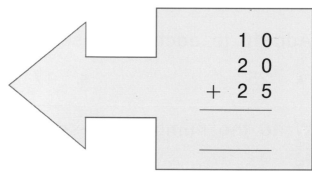

$$\begin{array}{r} 1\ 0 \\ 2\ 0 \\ +\ 2\ 5 \\ \hline \\ \hline \end{array}$$

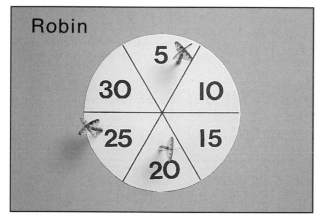

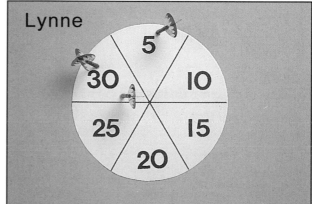

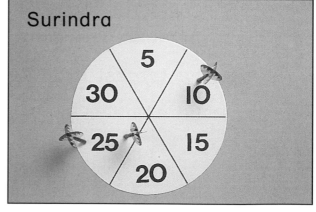

Who scored most?
Who scored least?

Assessment

Write these as numbers.

1. fourteen   **2.** thirty-five   **3.** forty

Add 10 to each of these.

4. 25   **5.** 17   **6.** 30

Write the numbers these abaci show.

7. 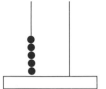   **8.** 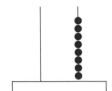   **9.**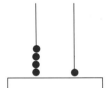

Draw three abaci. Show these numbers on them.

10. 37   **11.** 5   **12.** 60

13. Which number is 20 more than 12?

14. Which number is 10 less than 52? .

15. Which number is 1 more than 79?

16. Write the largest of these numbers.   41   27   39

17. Write the smallest of these numbers.   23   19   50

18.
$$\begin{array}{r} 4\,0 \\ +\ 1\,3 \\ \hline \\ \hline \end{array}$$

19.
$$\begin{array}{r} 5\,2 \\ +\ 1\,8 \\ \hline \\ \hline \end{array}$$

20.
$$\begin{array}{r} 3\,9 \\ +\ 4\,6 \\ \hline \\ \hline \end{array}$$